Getting by in
RUSSIAN

**A quick beginner's course
for tourists and businesspeople**

by
Thomas R. Beyer, Jr.
Dean, The Russian School
Middlebury College, Vermont

BARRON'S

New York / London / Toronto / Sydney

© Copyright 1986 by Barron's Educational Series, Inc.

All rights reserved
No part of this book may be reproduced in any form,
by photostat, microfilm, xerography, or any other
means, or incorporated into any information retrieval
system, electronic or mechanical, without the written
permission of the copyright owner.

All inquiries should be addressed to:
Barron's Educational Series, Inc.
250 Wireless Boulevard
Hauppauge, New York 11788

Paper Edition
International Standard Book No. 0-8120-2721-3
Library of Congress Catalog Card No. 86-10707

Library of Congress Cataloging-in-Publication Data

Beyer, Thomas R.
  Getting by in Russian.

    1. Russian language—Conversation and phrase books.
2. Russian language—Spoken Russian.   3. Russian
language—Text-books for English speakers.   I. Title.
PG2121.B48 1986   491.783′421   86-10707
ISBN 0-8120-2721-3 (pbk.)

Typesetting by Friedrich Typography, Santa Barbara
PRINTED IN THE UNITED STATES OF AMERICA

6789   987654321

Contents

The course . . .
and how to use it

Getting by in Russian is a course for anyone planning to visit the Soviet Union. It has been designed to give you a basic "survival kit" for some of the situations typical of a visit abroad.

"Getting by" means

- □ managing to keep your head above water
- □ having a chance to make yourself understood
- □ listening for clues so that you can get the gist of what's said
- □ knowing how to take shortcuts
- □ getting more fun out of your trip abroad

Each lesson

- □ concentrates on the language you'll need to speak and understand to cope with a particular situation—getting something to drink, finding your way around town, spending the evening at the theater, and so on.
- □ teaches you the minimum you'll need to "get by"— what you'll learn to speak has been carefully chosen so that it's simple to say and useful in a variety of situations.
- □ gives you many opportunities to repeat new words and expressions aloud and to answer simple questions.
- □ helps you pick out the key information in what people say to you, so that you can follow the general sense without worrying about the meaning of every word.

The set includes

☐ cassettes containing the basic "getting by" conversations

☐ a special section on how to make out the meaning of Russian signs

☐ texts of the conversations heard on the tapes

☐ a summary of what you'll need to say and listen for

☐ brief language notes

☐ self-testing exercises

☐ tips about the Soviet Union

☐ a reference section with a pronunciation guide, sections on numbers and prices, the days of the week, the months of the year, answers to the exercises, and Russian–English/English–Russian word lists.

To get the most from this course

Russian need not be hard to learn. Let your ear be the guide for your eye. You were able to understand and speak English before you learned the alphabet. The same can be true for Russian. Begin by listening to the tapes.

First, get used to the sound of Russian by listening to the first lesson on the cassette. As you listen, try to imitate the speaker as closely as possible. Don't be afraid to exaggerate at first; Russians are very expressive when they speak. Pronounce each word aloud; this will help you to remember it later. Keep working on the first program until you feel confident that you can say all the words and recognize all the letters. Now listen to the second lesson. When you have listened to the lesson once or twice, see if you can read the conversations in the text. Then test your progress with the exercises included in your text. Go back over the material until you feel comfortable with the entire lesson. Then go on to the third lesson, once again listening to the tape before you follow along in the book.

We all know the rule that "practice makes perfect." Vince Lombardi used to say that "practice doesn't make perfect; perfect practice makes perfect." Try to mimic the speakers as best you can. You'll be sounding like a real Russian in no time at all.

When you go abroad take this book with you, plus a good pocket dictionary.

If you can "get by in Russian," you'll enjoy your visit all the more.

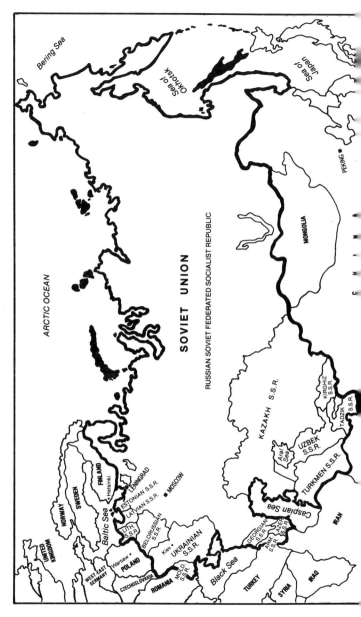

восемь

1 Getting by with Russian signs

When you get to the Soviet Union, one of your first and most striking impressions will surely be the alphabet. Russians use the Cyrillic alphabet, which has thirty-three characters. These characters or letters need not be confusing, especially if you take them one at a time. Many of the letters are the same in both Russian and English; others, taken from the Greek, may be familiar to you from mathematics or college fraternities. What remains is but a handful of unfamiliar ones.

The best way to learn these letters is to let your ear lead your eye. Listen to a word on the cassette, or say it the way it is given in the pronunciation guide. Repeat the word several times, and then look at the Russian spelling. How many letters are similar? How many are different? Finally, look at the English meaning of the word.

Pronunciation	Russian	English
dah	да	yes
nyet	нет	no
bahnk	банк	bank
bahr	бар	bar
pahrk	парк	park
ti-áhtr	театр	theater
káh-ssa	касса	cashier
tak-sée	такси	taxi
ki-óhsk	киоск	kiosk, newsstand
rista-ráhn	ресторан	restaurant
ka-féy	кафе	café
boo-fyét	буфет	buffet, coffee shop
mi-tróh	метро	metro, subway
ma-skváh	Москва	Moscow
intoo-réest	Интурист	Intourist
aira-póhrt	аэропорт	airport
aira-flóht	Аэрофлот	Aeroflot

Pronunciation	Russian	English
tili-fóhn	телефон	telephone
tooa-lyét	туалет	toilet, restroom
zahl	зал	hall
fkhot	вход	entrance
víy-khat	выход	exit
tsentr	центр	center
byoo-róh	бюро	bureau
gardi-róhp	гардероб	coat check, cloakroom
póhch-ta	почта	post office
ryat	ряд	row
stóy-ti	стойте	wait
myé-sta	место	place, seat
soovi-née-ry	сувениры	souvenirs
nye koo-réet	Не курить	No smoking
bal-shóy	большой	Bolshoi, big
zhén-skiy	женский	female, ladies'
moosh-skóy	мужской	male, men's
pée-va	пиво	beer
lyé-nin	Ленин	Lenin
yi-shóh	ещё	more, else

A few notes about Russian pronunciation and the alphabet are in order. Like all alphabets, the Russian one is at best an approximation of what is said. The spelling of some words may differ from what we expect on the basis of pronunciation. It will help if you keep the following guidelines in mind.

1   Several Russian consonants can be pronounced in two ways. Normally they are hard, like the "n" in "note." But sometime they are soft, like the "n" in "onion." Soft letters are indicated by writing the consonant followed by a "y."

2   When an "o" is not accented, it is normally pronounced as "a" or "ah," as in "stop."

3   When an "e" is not accented, it is often pronounced like an "i" in "missing."

2 Getting to meet people

Conversations

These conversations are heard on the taped programs. After listening to the tape once or twice, try to read the printed text. Repeat the words and phrases you hear on the tape as closely as possible. After reading the conversations, look at the language summary and explanations, then repeat the conversations.

Native speakers often use more words than necessary to communicate their thoughts. For you to "get by," you need concentrate only on the most important words and phrases, which are set in **bold letters** for your convenience.

Ordering a cup of coffee

Guest	**Молодой человек!**
Waiter	Здравствуйте. Что вы хотите?
Guest	Дайте мне чашку **кофе, пожалуйста.**
Waiter	Вот ваш кофе.
Guest	**Спасибо.**
Waiter	Пожалуйста.

Дайте мне чашку кофе, пожалуйста.	Give me a cup of coffee, please.

Ordering a bottle of wine

Bartender	Добрый вечер.
Customer	**Добрый вечер. У вас есть вино?**
Bartender	Да. Вы хотите красное или белое?
Customer	**Белое** сухое?
Bartender	Сухое. Оно очень хорошее.
Customer	**Хорошо. Я возьму** белое.

У вас есть вино?	Do you have any wine?
Вы хотите красное или белое?	Do you want red or white?
Белое сухое?	Is the white (wine) dry?
Хорошо. Я возьму белое.	OK. I'll take some white (wine).

Ordering a mixed drink

Guest	**Девушка, у вас есть тоник?**
Waitress	К сожалению, нет.
Guest	**А сок есть?**
Waitress	Есть. Хотите водку с соком?
Guest	**Да, водка с соком, пожалуйста.**
Waitress	Сейчас принесу.

| Водка с соком, пожалуйста. | A screwdriver, please. |
| Сейчас принесу. | I'll bring it right away. |

Paying the bill

Customer	**Молодой человек, сколько с меня?**
Bartender	Пиво и водка с соком, да?
Customer	**Нет. Джин с тоником и водка с соком.**
Bartender	Четыре доллара.

Сколько с меня?	How much do I owe?
водка с соком	a vodka with juice (screwdriver)
джин с тоником	a gin and tonic

Language summary

What you need to say

How to say "Hello" . . .

Здравствуйте *(Zdráhstvuyti)*	*any time of day*
Доброе утро *(Dóhbrayi óotra)*	*in the morning*
Добрый день *(Dóhbriy dyen)*	*in the afternoon*
Добрый вечер *(Dóhbriy vyéchir)*	*in the evening*

and "Goodbye"

До свидания *(Da svidáhniya)*

How to say "Please" or "You're welcome" . . .

Пожалуйста (*Pazháhlasta*)

and "Thank-you"

Спасибо (*Spaséeba*)

How to order something to drink

пиво (*péeva*)	a beer
шампанское (*shampáhnskayi*)	champagne
кофе (*kóhfi*)	coffee
коньяк (*kanyák*)	cognac
сок (*sohk*)	juice
лимонад (*limanáht*)	a soft drink
водка (*vóhtka*)	vodka
вино (*vinóh*)	wine

How to order another one . . .

Ещё один. (*Yishóh adéen.*)

or two more

Ещё два. (*Yishóh dvah.*)

How to call the waiter

Молодой человек (*Maladóy chilavyék.*)

. . . or waitress

Девушка. (*Dyévooshka.*)

How to ask for the bill

Сколько с меня? (*Skóhlka s minyá?*)

What you need to listen for

Being asked what you want . . .

Что вы хотите? (*Shtoh vy khatéeti?*)

and how you want it

Как вы хотите? (*Kahk vy khatéeti?*)

"We have it"

У нас есть. (*Oo nahs yest.*)

"We don't have it"

У нас нет. (*Oo nahs nyet.*)

Explanations

In Russian the nouns for people are either masculine or feminine. Objects can be masculine, feminine, or neuter. Masculine words normally end in a consonant, like the **к** in **сок** (*sohk*). Feminine words end in the vowel **а** or **я**. Neuter nouns have **о** or **е** for an ending. Plurals of many Russian nouns are formed by adding **ы** or **и**.

The endings of Russian nouns change according to a word's role in the sentence. For example, the words **водка** (*vóhtka*) and **сок** (*sohk*) become **водку с соком** (*vóhtkoo s sóhkam*) when a Russian wants a screwdriver (literally, "vodka with juice"). Since the basic meaning of the word remains unchanged, you should be able to "get by" without worrying too much about these endings.

Numbers are important for "getting by." You need them for dealing with prices, time, phone numbers, your room key, paying the bill, etc.

1	один (*adéen*)	**6**	шесть (*shest*)
2	два (*dvah*)	**7**	семь (*syem*)
3	три (*tree*)	**8**	восемь (*vóhsim*)
4	четыре (*chitýri*)	**9**	девять (*dyévit*)
5	пять (*pyat*)	**10**	десять (*dyésit*)

Exercises

1   Can you respond to the following situations?

    a   Вы хотите сок? (*Vy khatéeti sohk?*)   You love juice; say "Yes please."

    b   Вы хотите водку с соком? (*Vy khatéeti vóhtkoo s sóhkam?*)   You can't stand vodka; say, "No, thank you."

    c   Ещё пиво? (*Yishóh péeva?*) You've already had enough beer.

2   You've just asked, "What do they have?" You hear: У нас есть пиво. (*Oo nahs yest péeva.*)   Do they have

    a   wine?   **b**   beer?   **c**   screwdrivers?

You hear: У нас нет кофе. (*Oo nahs nyet kóhfi.*) Are they out of

    a   cognac?   **b**   vodka?   **c**   coffee?

You hear: Джин с тоником. (*Dzhin s tóhnikam.*) Is that a

    a   glass of wine?   **b**   bottle of beer?
    c   gin and tonic?

3   **a**   Say "Hello" to the bartender. Order a cup of coffee.
    b   You've just returned to your hotel after the ballet. Try to get the waitress's attention. Order a screwdriver and a cognac.

    c   Say "Good evening" to your waiter and ask him if he has any beer. Order two of them.

4   **a**   The bartender says he has both red and white wine. Tell him you'll have some dry white wine.
    b   The first gin and tonic hit the spot. Order another one.
    c   Can you get his attention and pay the bill?

5 Complete the following equations.

a два (*dvah*) + один (*adéen*) = _____.

b шесть (*shest*) + три (*tree*) = _____.

c восемь (*vóhsim*) − семь (*syem*) = _____.

d десять (*dyésit*) − четыре (*chitýri*) = _____.

e девять (*dyévit*) − пять (*pyat*) = _____.

It's worth knowing

Greetings

In the Soviet Union people use the word **Здравствуйте** (*Zdráhstvuyti*) to greet one another. Since the expression literally means "Be healthy," you normally say it to each individual only once a day. If you meet the same person a second time, you might want to say **Доброе утро** (*Dóhbrayi óotra*) for "Good morning," **Добрый день** (*Dóhbriy dyen*) for "Good afternoon," or **Добрый вечер** (*Dóhbriy vyéchir*) for "Good evening." When you are leaving, it is proper to say **До свидания** (*Da svidáhniya*).

Addressing people

If you are trying to get someone's attention, you may use **Молодой человек** (*Maladóy chilavyék*) for a young man and **Девушка** (*Dyévooshka*) for a young woman. In business meetings it is quite alright to use "Mister" plus the individual's last name. Most Russians (such as your guide, driver, etc.) will probably introduce themselves by their first names—e.g., Natasha (**Наташа**) or Viktor (**Виктор**). In speaking to one another, Russians may use the first name plus another name (e.g., Ivan Ivanovich). If you have read any Russian novels, you're probably familiar with this second name, called a *patronymic*, which is formed from the father's first name.

If you want to ask someone's name, simply say: **Как вас зовут?** (*Kahk vahs zavóot?*).

Saying "Please" and "Thank-you"

The most common way to say "Thank-you" is **спасибо** (*spaséeba*). You may also hear **спасибо большое** (*spaséeba balshóhyi)* or **большое спасибо** (*balshóhyi spaséeba*). **Спасибо** may also be used to refuse something politely, much as we say in English, "No, thank you (**Нет, спасибо**/*Nyet, spaséeba*). To say "Please," we use the word **пожалуйста** (*pazháhlasta*). This word is also used to accept something offered to you and to say "You're welcome."

At the bar

Your Intourist hotel will probably have a bar where you can order a variety of beverages. In most cases you will pay for them in dollars or some other hard currency. You may want to order a beer (**пиво**/*péeva*), which might be a can of imported German or Dutch beer. You can also order a bottle of Soviet champagne (**шампанское** /*shampáhnskayi*). Most people prefer the semidry sort (**полусухое**/*paloosookhóhyi*). The Soviet Union also produces several fine wines. The ones from the southern republics, such as Georgia, can be excellent. Ask your bartender if he has a bottle of red (**красное**/ *kráhsnayi*) or, white (**белое**/*byélayi*) wine. Georgian or French cognac (**коньяк**₁/*kanyák*) may also be available, but make sure you check out the vodka (**водка**/*vóhtka*). Russians like to drink it neat, but you might want to mix it with tonic (**тоник**/*tóhnik*) or some sort of juice (**сок**/*sohk*). If you prefer something nonalcoholic, you might have some mineral water (**минеральная вода**/*miniráhlnaya vadáh*) or a fruit-flavored soft drink (**лимонад**/*limanáht*). Many bars offer a good cup of demitasse coffee (**кофе**/ *kóhfi*). If you want it with sugar, say **кофе с сахаром** (*kóhfi s sáhkharam*).

МОСКВА

3 Getting by in your hotel

Conversations

Checking in

Guest	**Здравствуйте. Меня зовут** Смит.
Administrator	Добрый день, Мистер Смит. Ваш паспорт, пожалуйста.
Guest	Вот **мой паспорт.**
Administrator	Номер 120.
Guest	**На каком этаже** этот номер?
Administrator	На шестом. Лифт вон там.

На каком этаже этот номер?   What floor is that room on?

Getting your key

Guest	**Добрый вечер.**
Attendant	Добрый вечер. Чем вам помочь?
Guest	Дайте мне, пожалуйста **ключ от номера** 120.
Attendant	Покажите мне ваш пропуск, пожалуйста. Вот ваш ключ.
Guest	**Спасибо.**
Attendant	Пожалуйста.

Дайте мне, пожалуйста, ключ от номера 120.   Give me the key to room 120, please.

Вот ваш ключ.   Here is your key.

Finding the buffet

Guest	**Доброе утро. Скажите, пожалуйста, где здесь буфет?**
Attendant	Он на втором этаже.
Guest	**Повторите, пожалуйста.**
Attendant	На втором этаже.

Где здесь буфет?	Where is the coffee shop?
Он на втором этаже.	It's on the second floor.

Ordering breakfast

Guest	**Кефир, пожалуйста.**
Server	Кефир, хорошо. Что ещё?
Guest	**Сосиски есть?**
Server	Сосисок нет.
Guest	**Тогда дайте мне яичницу, пожалуйста.**
Server	Вот вам яичница. Вы хотите кофе или чай?
Guest	**Кофе с молоком.**

Сосиски есть?	Are there any hot dogs?
Тогда дайте мне яичницу.	Then give me some fried eggs.

At the bank

Guest	**Здесь можно обменять валюту?**
Teller	Да, можно. Дайте мне вашу декларацию, пожалуйста.
Guest	**Я хочу обменять доллары.**
Teller	Сколько вы хотите обменять?
Guest	**Двадцать.**
Teller	Распишитесь, пожалуйста. Вот ваша декларация и рубли.
Guest	**Спасибо. До свидания.**
Teller	Молодой человек, не забудьте вашу квитанцию.

Здесь можно обменять валюту?	Can I exchange foreign currency here?
Вот ваша декларация.	Here is your declaration.
Не забудьте вашу квитанцию.	Don't forget your receipt.

Language summary

What you need to say

Where is ...

Где мой номер? (*Gdye moy nóhmir?*)	my room?
Где буфет? (*Gdye boofyét?*)	the coffee shop?
Где банк? (*Gdye bahnk?*)	the bank?

Asking for ...

Мой ключ, пожалуйста. (*Moy klyooch, pazháhlasta.*)	your key.
Яичница, пожалуйста. (*Yaéechnitsa, pazháhlasta.*)	fried eggs.
Кофе с молоком, пожалуйста. (*Kóhfi s malakóhm, pazháhlasta.*)	coffee with milk.
Чай с сахаром, пожалуйста. (*Chay s sáhkharam, pazháhlasta.*)	tea with sugar.
Чай без сахара, пожалуйста. (*Chay byes sáhkhara, pazháhlasta.*)	tea without sugar.

If you don't understand

Повторите, пожалуйста. (*Paftaréeti, pazháhlasta.*)	Could you repeat that?
Ещё раз. (*Yishóh ras.*)	One more time.
Медленнее, пожалуйста. (*Myédliniyi, pazháhlasta.*)	A little slower, please.

What to listen for

Being asked for ...

Ваш паспорт. (*Vahsh páhspart.*)	your passport.
Ваш пропуск. (*Vahsh próhpoosk.*)	your hotel pass.
Ваша декларация.	your declaration.
(*Váhsha diklaráhtsiya.*)	

Which floor?

На первом этаже.	On the first.
(*Na pyérvam etazhé.*)	
На втором этаже.	On the second.
(*Na ftaróhm etazhé.*)	
На третьем этаже.	On the third.
(*Na tryétim etazhé.*)	

Explanations

One of the most important things that you can learn in a foreign language is the number system. You have already seen in Lesson 2 that numbers are essential if you are to understand prices. In this lesson you need numbers to get your room key, ask what floor you're on, and change money.

The Russian number system is very similar to English. Just as English has two sets of numbers—ordinal and cardinal—so does the Russian system. We say "one," but the "first" floor; "two," but the "second" floor, etc. After "three" and "third" the two sets are so similar that they are easily recognizable. The same is true for Russian.

It is important to learn the first four ordinal numbers:

первый (*pyérviy*)	first
второй (*ftaróy*)	second
третий (*tryétiy*)	third
четвёртый (*chitvyórtiy*)	fourth

After that it should be a simple matter to understand the other ordinal numbers. Look how closely the two sets are related:

пять (*pyat*)	пятый (*pyátiy*)
шесть (*shest*)	шестой (*shistóy*)
семь (*syem*)	седьмой (*sidmóy*)
восемь (*vóhsim*)	восьмой (*vasmóy*)
девять (*dyévit*)	девятый (*divyátiy*)
десять (*dyésit*)	десятый (*disyátiy*)

You'll also want to learn the next ten cardinal numbers, from eleven to twenty. Notice that they all end in the letters **-надцать** (*-natsat*), a contracted form. Originally, these numbers were formed by putting "one on ten," "two on ten," etc.

11 одиннадцать (*adéenatsat*)
12 двенадцать (*dvináhtsat*)
13 тринадцать (*trináhtsat*)
14 четырнадцать (*chitýrnatsat*)
15 пятнадцать (*pitnáhtsat*)
16 шестнадцать (*shisnáhtsat*)
17 семнадцать (*simnáhtsat*)
18 восемнадцать (*vasimnáhtsat*)
19 девятнадцать (*divitnáhtsat*)
20 двадцать (*dváhtsat*)

Exercises

Tourist	Добрый вечер. (*Dóhbriy vyéchir.*)
	Меня зовут Ричардс. (*Minyá zavóot Réecharts.*)
Receptionist	Ваш паспорт, пожалуйста. (*Vahsh páhspart, pazháhlasta.*)
	Номер девятнадцать (*Nóhmir divitnáhtsat*) на третьем этаже. (*na tryétim etazhé.*)
Tourist	Повторите, пожалуйста, на каком этаже? (*Paftaréeti, pazháhlasta, na kakóhm etazhé?*)
Receptionist	На третьем. (*Na tryétim.*)

1 Answer the following questions in English.
   a What is the tourist's name?
   b What room is he given?
   c Which floor is the room on?

2 In a big hotel, where you pick up the key on the floor, you need say only the last two digits of your room to get the key. Thus 1804 becomes simply: Номер четыре, пожалуйста. (*Nóhmir chitýri, pazháhlasta.*) Can you get the key

   a for room 1117?
   b for your colleagues in room 1105?
   c for the tongue-tied American in room 1112?

3. At the bank, when you are asked, Что вы хотите обменять? (*Shtóh vy khatéeti abminyát?*), do you answer

   a фунты (*fóonty*)?
   b доллары (*dóhllary*)?
   c марки (*máhrki*)?

When the teller asks for your декларация (*diklaráhtsiya*), do you give her

   a your passport?
   b your customs declaration?
   c your visa?

When she says, Распишитесь, пожалуйста
(*Raspishútis, pazháhlasta*), do you

a sign the receipt?
b take your money?
c give her your passport?

4 You want to order a breakfast of juice, fried eggs, and a cup of tea. How do you reply to the following questions?

a *Server*   Доброе утро. (*Dóhbrayi óotra.*)
             Вы хотите сок или кефир?
             (*Vy khatéeti sohk éeli kiféer?*)

     You   _____.

b *Server*   Хорошо. (*Kharashóh.*) Что ещё?
             (*Shtoh yishóh?*) Сосиски или яичница?
             (*Saséeski éeli yaéechnitsa?*)

     You   _____.

c *Server*   Кофе или чай? (*Kóhfi éeli chay?*)

     You   _____.

5 On which floor are the following located?
(Answer in English.)

a Банк на четвёртом этаже.
      (*Bahnk na chitvyórtam etazhé.*)
b Буфет на седьмом этаже.
      (*Boofyét na sidmóhm etazhé.*)
c Мужской туалет на втором этаже.
      (*Mooshskóy tooalyét na ftaróhm etazhé.*)
d Ресторан на одиннадцатом этаже.
      (*Ristaráhn na adéenatsatam etazhé.*)
e Ваш номер на шестом этаже.
      (*Vahsh nóhmir na shistóhm etazhé.*)

It's worth knowing

Accommodations

You will probably be traveling to the Soviet Union with a tourist agency, or your visit will be sponsored by one of the Soviet trade or educational agencies. In many cases you will probably not get to pick the hotel in which you will stay. If you are traveling under the auspices of Intourist (**Интурист**), you can guarantee the accommodations according to the price that you are willing to pay. These can be either first class or deluxe.

At the airport your group will be met by a representative of the hosting agency. If you are traveling alone, you can check in at the Intourist desk, where they will have your hotel assignment ready and provide you with transportation to the hotel.

At the hotel you (or your tour guide) will present a voucher for travel, along with your passport and visa, at the reception desk. You should remember to retrieve your passport and visa before you depart. You will be given a pass (**пропуск**/*próhpoosk*) or sometimes simply a card (**карточка**/*káhrtachka*) with the name of the hotel on it and your room number. You then proceed to the floor, where someone is on duty around the clock. In most hotels this attendant (**дежурная**/*dizhóornaya*) will give you your key. Besides holding on to your key, she can make you tea, wake you up, bring you an extra blanket, etc. It's a good idea to make friends with her.

Getting breakfast

If you are with a group, almost all of your meals will be arranged for you. If you are traveling alone, you'll probably have to get breakfast for yourself. At some hotels there is a restaurant where, for a set price, you can help yourself to a smorgasbord (**шведский стол**/*shvétskiy stohl*). Otherwise you can go to the (**буфет**/*boofyét*), a cross between a coffee shop and a snack bar. There should be a selection of items, including bread (**хлеб**/(*khlep*), butter (**масло**/*máhsla*), cheese (**сыр**/*syr*), salami (**колбаса**/*kalbasáh*), and a yogurt-like drink (**кефир**/ *kiféer*). There should also be some warm dishes, such as fried eggs (**яичница**/*yaéechnitsa*), hard-boiled eggs (**яйца**/*yátsah*), and maybe even hot dogs (**сосиски**/ *saséeski*), which seem to be a Russian favorite for breakfast. Of course, you'll find juice (**сок**/*sohk*) and plenty of tea (**чай**/*chay*) and coffee (**кофе**/*kóhfi*).

Exchanging currency

Russians are very strict about exchanging money, and you should be careful to follow the proper procedures. When you enter the country, you will fill out a declaration (**декларация**/*diklaráhtsiya*) listing all the foreign currency, travelers' checks, etc., in your possession. Note that it is illegal to bring Soviet currency obtained outside the country into the Soviet Union. Your declaration will be stamped and initialed by a customs agent upon your arrival.

You should keep this document because you will need it to exchange money at banks and official exchange points. When you do exchange money the first time, the transaction will be entered on your declaration. You will also be asked to sign a receipt (**квитанция**/*kvitáhntsiya*), of which you will be given a copy. It is important to keep these and the declaration to exchange any unused Soviet currency back into dollars, which you must do before leaving the country.

You will be able to pay in dollars for some items at special stores called *Beriozka* (**Берёзка**). These stores are found in major tourist hotels and at other selected locations. You may already know of the hard currency bars in some tourist hotels. In all other establishments, you must pay in Soviet currency, i.e., rubles and kopecks.

4 Getting your shopping done

Conversations

At the post office

Customer	**Здравствуйте. У вас есть открытки?**
Clerk	Да есть. Вот они. Посмотрите.
Customer	**Сколько стоит** открытка в Америку?
Clerk	Тридцать пять копеек.
Customer	**Хорошо. Я** возьму эту открытку и **марок на тридцать пять копеек.**
Clerk	Пожалуйста, ваша открытка и ваши марки.

У вас есть открытки?	Do you have any postcards?
Сколько стоит открытка в Америку?	How much does a postcard to America cost?
Тридцать пять копеек.	Thirty-five kopecks.

Customer	Я хочу послать **авиаписьмо** в Америку.
Clerk	Авиаписьмо в Америку стоит сорок пять копеек.
Customer	**У вас есть конверты?**
Clerk	Да. Пожалуйста. Возьмите конверт и марки. Сорок семь копеек, пожалуйста.

At the bookstore

Customer	Девушка, **покажите мне,** пожалуйста, эту книгу.
Clerk	Какую? Эту книгу?

Customer	**Нет.** Не эту, а ту.
Clerk	Пожалуйста. Платите в кассу один рубль тридцать копеек.

Покажите мне, пожалуйста, эту книгу.	Show me that book, please.
Платите в кассу один рубль тридцать копеек.	Pay one ruble and thirty kopecks at the cashier's.

At the cashier's booth

Customer	Первый отдел. **Один рубль тридцать копеек.**
Cashier	Вот ваш чек и сдача.
Customer	**Спасибо.**
Cashier	Пожалуйста.

Первый отдел.	The first department.
Вот ваш чек и сдача.	Here is your receipt and change.

At the service counter

Customer	Девушка. Вот вам **чек.**
Clerk	Вам завернуть?
Customer	**Да, пожалуйста.**
Clerk	Вот ваша книга. До свидания.

Вам завернуть?	Should I wrap it for you?

At the Beriozka

Customer	У вас есть **американские сигареты?**
Clerk	Да есть. Кент, Марлборо, Винстон.
Customer	Я возьму **один блок Марлборо. Выпишите мне, пожалуйста,** один блок.
Clerk	Как вы будете платить? Долларами?
Customer	Да. **У меня доллары.**

Я возьму один блок Марлборо.	I'll take a carton of Marlboro.
Выпишите мне, пожалуйста, один блок.	Write me out an order for one carton.
Как вы будете платить? Долларами?	How are you going to pay? In dollars?

Language summary

What you need to say

Saying what you want ...

марки (*máhrki*)	stamps
открытки (*atkrýtki*)	postcards
конверт (*kanvyért*)	an envelope
книга (*knéega*)	a book
сигареты (*sigaryéty*)	cigarettes

and asking how much it costs

Сколько стоят марки?
  (*Skóhlka stóhit máhrki?*)
Сколько стоят открытки?
  (*Skóhlka stóhit atkrýtki?*)
Сколько стоит конверт?
  (*Skóhlka stóhit kanvyért?*)
Сколько стоит книга?
  (*Skóhlka stóhit knéega?*)
Сколько стоят сигареты?
  (*Skóhlka stóhit sigaryéty?*)

What you need to listen for

Платите в кассу.   Pay at the cashier's.
   (*Platéeti f kássoo.*)
Вам завернуть?   Do you want it wrapped?
   (*Vahm zavirnóot?*)
Вот ваш чек . . .   Here is your receipt . . .
   (*Voht vahsh chyek*)
и сдача. (*ee zdáhcha.*)   and your change.

Being told they don't have any

У нас нет. (*Oo nahs nyet.*)
К сожалению, нет. (*K sazhalyéniyoo, nyet.*).

Explanations

The plurals of most Russian masculine and feminine
nouns are formed by the endings **ы** or **и**. Look at the
following examples:

Singular	Plural
конверт (*kanvyért*)	конверты (*kanvyérty*)
сигарета (*sigaryéta*)	сигареты (*sigaryéty*)
марка (*máhrka*)	марки (*máhrki*)
открытка (*atkrýtka*)	открытки (*atkrýtki*)
книга (*knéega*)	книги (*knéegi*)

The plurals of most neuter nouns end with **a** or **e**.

Singular	Plural
авиаписьмо (*aviapismóh*)	авиаписьма (*aviapéesma*)
место (*myésta*)	места (*mistáh*)

The choice between **ы** or **и** and **a** or **я** is based on several
spelling rules, which you need not learn. The plurals of
those nouns that you are likely to need are listed after their
singular forms in the English-Russian word list.

It is important that you be able to recognize when people are talking to you or asking you a question. In English the pronoun "you" does not change forms. In Russian the word for "you" is **вы** (*vy*), but it may take other forms, such as **вам** (*vahm*) or **вас** (*vahs*).

You have actually seen and heard all of these forms. Do you remember the following sentences?

Вам завернуть?	Should I wrap it for you?
(*Vahm zavirnóot?*)	
Как вас зовут?	What's your name?
(*Kahk vahs zavóot?*)	(What do they call you?)

Here are some more numbers:

20	двадцать	(*dváhtsat*)
30	тридцать	(*tréetsat*)
40	сорок	(*sóhrak*)
50	пятьдесят	(*pitdisyát*)
60	шестьдесят	(*shisdisyát*)
70	семьдесят	(*syémdisit*)
80	восемьдесят	(*vóhsimdisit*)
90	девяносто	(*divinóhsta*)
100	сто	(*stoh*)

The number "twenty-one" in Russian is **двадцать один** (*dváhtsat adéen*). "Twenty-two" is **двадцать два** (*dváhtsat dvah*) and so on.

Numbers also appear in prices. Russian words take different forms after numbers. Thus you would say **один рубль** (*adéen roobl*), but **два** (*dvah*), **три** (*tree*), **четыре рубля** (*chitýri rooblyá*). For the numbers five through twenty, you would say **пять рублей** (*pyat rooblyéy*), and so on.

The word for kopecks undergoes a similar change: **Одна копейка** (*Adnáh kapyéyka*), **две** (*dvye*), **три** (*tree*), **четыре копейки** (*chitýri kapyéyki*), but **пять копеек** (*pyat kapyéik*). Note that the number 2 has one form for masculine nouns (**два**/*dvah*) and one for feminine nouns (**две** /*dvye*.)

Exercises

1 Match the correct prices with the following items:
45 к., 87 к., 1 р. 13 к., 3 р. 25 к., 6 р. 48 к.

    a Эта книга стоит три рубля двадцать пять копеек. (*Éhta knéega stóhit tree rooblyá dváhtsat pyat kapyéik.*)

    b Авиаписьмо стоит сорок пять копеек. (*Aviapismóh stóhit sóhrak pyat kapyéik.*)

    c Эти открытки стоят один рубль тринадцать копеек. (*Éhti atkrýtki stóhit adéen roobl trináhtsat kapyéik.*)

    d Сигареты и вино стоят шесть рублей сорок восемь копеек. (*Sigaryéty ee vinóh stóhit shest rooblyéy sóhrak vóhsim kapyéik.*)

    e Яичница стоит восемьдесят семь копеек. (*Yaéechnitsa stóhit vóhsimdisit syem kapyéik.*)

2 Jot down the following prices to show to the cashier. For example, два рубля десять копеек (*dvah rooblyá dyésit kapyéik*) 2 р. 10 к.

    a три рубля (*tree rooblyá*)

    b десять рублей двадцать копеек (*dyésit rooblyéy dvahtsat kapyéik*)

    c шестьдесят копеек (*shisdisyát kapyéik*)

    d один рубль пятьдесят копеек (*adéen roobl pitdisyát kapyéik*)

    e восемь рублей девяносто копеек (*vóhsim rooblyéy divinóhsta kapyéik*)

3 Some of the members of your group have just discovered that you can speak a little Russian. Can you help them at the kiosk?

    a Mrs. Brown needs some postcards. Ask the salesgirl if she has any.

    b Mrs. Brown says she'll take them. She also needs some stamps.

c Mr. James wants to know how much the Moscow
 guidebook costs. Can you inquire for him?

 d Mr. Richards wants to try some Russian cigarettes.
 Find out if they have any and how much they cost.

4 You're adding up your expenses for the day. You've
completed the list and are just beginning to fill in the
prices. Look again at the conversations at the post office
and bookstore and total your purchases.

postcard   *15 к.*
stamps
airmail envelope
book

total   ———

It's worth knowing

Making purchases

At the kiosk (**киоск**/*kióhsk*) in your hotel, you should be
able to purchase stamps (**марки**/*máhrki*) as well as
postcards (**открытки**/*atkrýtki*) and envelopes (**конверты**
/*kanvyérty*). They will also have a selection of Russian
cigarettes (**сигареты**/*sigaryéty*), newspapers (**газеты**/
gazyéty), and magazines (**журналы**/*zhoornáhly*). Some
Intourist hotels may have copies of the *International
Herald Tribune,* but you will probably have to ask for it.

At most Russian stores you first go to a counter where you may inspect the items for sale. Don't hesitate to ask to see something. Here one little word—**это** (*éhta*) "this"—and your finger can be very handy. Simply say, **Покажите мне это, пожалуйста** (*Pakazhíti mnye éhta, pazháhlasta.*)—Show me this, please. The salesperson will be happy to oblige you. If you decide to buy the item, you must go to one of the cashier's booths, where you tell them the section of the store (first, second, etc.) and the amount of the purchase. When you have paid, you will be given a receipt (**чек**); bring it back to the original counter, where you can claim your purchase. Don't forget to have them wrap it up for you.

Prices in Russian stores are given in rubles and kopecks. There are 100 kopecks in one ruble—much like the pennies in a dollar. A ruble is worth about $1.35. Often the prices are written as follows:

1 р. 37 к. (one ruble, thirty-seven kopecks)

If you can't understand the price, have the attendant write it out for you on a piece of paper. She'll appreciate the fact that you tried. Tell her, **Напишите это, пожалуйста.** (*Napishíti éhta, pazháhlasta.*)

Beriozka stores

The Beriozkas are a chain of stores that accept only foreign currency (**валюта** /*valyóota*), such as dollars, pounds, marks, and francs. Prices on many items are somewhat less expensive than in regular stores, and often there is a better selection. Some are self-service stores, where you gather your purchases in a shopping cart or basket and proceed to the checkout counter. In others you will have to have the salesclerk show you the items and then write out the order, which you take to the cashier to pay. In any case, you will be asked what currency you will be paying with. The answer will include the country as well as the type of currency: "American dollars" (**американские доллары**/ *amirikáhnskiyi dóhllary*).

5 Getting around town

Conversations

Asking for the center of town

Tourist	**Извините, пожалуйста. Где находится центр?**
Passerby	Вон там. Идите прямо.
Tourist	**Спасибо большое.**

Извините, пожалуйста.	Excuse me, please.
Где находится . . . ?	Where is . . . ?

How to get to the National restaurant

Tourist	**Скажите, пожалуйста, как пройти в ресторан «Националь»?**
Policeman	Идите прямо, а потом налево. Вы сразу его увидите.

Как пройти . . . ?	How can I get to . . . ?
Вы сразу его увидите.	You'll see it right away.

How to get to the circus

Tourist	Вы не знаете, **как проехать в цирк?**
Receptionist	Туда нужно ехать на метро.
Tourist	**До какой станции?**
Receptionist	До станции «Университетская».

Как проехать . . . ?	How can I get (by vehicle) to . . . ?
Туда нужно ехать на метро.	You have to take the subway.
До какой станции?	To which station?

Taking a taxi

Driver	Вам куда?
Passenger	Я хочу попасть **в гостиницу «Россия»**.
Driver	Приехали. Три рубля десять копеек.
Passenger	Вот вам **три рубля пятьдесят копеек**.
Driver	Спасибо вам. До свидания.

Вам куда?	Where do you want to go?
В гостиницу «Россия».	To the Rossiya Hotel.

Ordering a car

Guest	**Я хочу заказать машину на завтра.**
Clerk	Хорошо. На какое время?
Guest	**На девять часов.**
Clerk	Куда вы едете?
Guest	**В американское посольство.**
Clerk	Хорошо. Приходите завтра в девять часов.

Я хочу заказать машину на завтра.	I want to order a car for tomorrow.
На какое время?	For what time?
Куда вы едете?	Where are you going?
Приходите завтра в девять часов.	Come tomorrow at nine o'clock.

Guest	**Мне нужна машина.**
Receptionist	Хорошо. Когда нужна?
Guest	**Сегодня, в три часа.**
Receptionist	Куда?
Guest	**В аэропорт «Шереметьево».**
Receptionist	Машина будет вас ждать.

Мне нужна машина.	I need a car.
Машина будет вас ждать.	A car will be waiting for you.

Language summary

What you need to say

Getting someone's attention

Извините, пожалуйста. (*Izvinéeti, pazháhlasta.*)
  Excuse me, please.
Скажите, пожалуйста. (*Skazhíti, pazháhlasta.*)
  Tell me, please.

Asking for information

Где (*Gdye*)
  Where is . . .?
Как пройти (*Kahk praytée*)
  How can I get to . . .?
Как проехать (*Kahk prayékhat*)
  How can I get (by vehicle) to . . .?

Ordering a car

Я хочу заказать машину. (*Ya khachóo zakazáht mashinoo.*)
  I want to order a car.
Мне нужна машина. (*Mnye noozhnáh mashína.*)
  I need a car.

Telling the driver where to go

В гостиницу «Россия». (*V gastéenitsoo "Rasséeya."*)
  To the Rossiya Hotel.
В ресторан «Националь». (*V ristaráhn "Natsianáhl."*)
  To the National restaurant.
В аэропорт «Шереметьево». (*V airapóhrt "Shirimyétiva."*)
  To Sheremetyevo Airport.
На Красную площадь. (*Na Kráhsnooyoo plóhshat.*)
  To Red Square.

When you want the car

сегодня (*sivóhdnya*)	today
завтра (*záhftra*)	tomorrow
утром (*óotram*)	in the morning
днём (*dnyom*)	in the afternoon
вечером (*vyéchiram*)	in the evening

What you need to listen for

Directions

прямо (*pryáma*)	straight ahead
направо (*napráhva*)	to the right
налево (*nalyéva*)	to the left

Questions

Куда?(*Koodáh?*)	Where to?
Когда? (*Kagdáh?*)	When?

Explanations

Russians have two ways of asking how to get from one place to another. If you are on foot, you ask, **Как пройти?** (*Kahk praytée?*) If you intend to go by car, taxi, or another means of transportation, you ask, **Как проехать?** (*Kahk prayékhat?*)

There are also two ways to say "to" in Russian. Most words use the preposition **в**.

в аэропорт (*v airapóhrt*)	to the airport
в ресторан (*v ristaráhn*)	to the restaurant
в цирк (*f tsirk*)	to the circus
в театр (*f tiáhtr*)	to the theater
в гостиницу (*v gastéenitsoo*)	to the hotel

A few words use **на**. Some of the more common combinations you might use are:

на почту	to the post office
(*na póhchtoo*)	
на Красную площадь	to Red Square
(*na Kráhsnooyoo plóhshat*)	
на станцию метро	to the metro station
(*na stáhntsiyoo mitróh*)	

You'll certainly want to be able to tell time in Russian. You already know the numbers. See how they combine with the Russian word for "o'clock" (**час**/*chahs*):

1:00	час (*chahs*)
2:00	два часа (*dvah chasáh*)
3:00	три часа (*tree chasáh*)
4:00	четыре часа (*chitýri chasáh*)
5:00	пять часов (*pyat chasóhf*)
6:00	шесть часов (*shest chasóhf*)
7:00	семь часов (*syem chasóhf*)
8:00	восемь часов (*vóhsim chasóhf*)
9:00	девять часов (*dyévit chasóhf*)
10:00	десять часов (*dyésit chasóhf*)
11:00	одиннадцать часов (*adéenatsat chasóhf*)
12:00	двенадцать часов (*dvináhtsat chasóhf*)

Russians often use the twenty-four hour clock for transportation schedules, times of theater performances, and for listing opening and closing times of stores, cafés, etc. Thus "1:00 P.M." is sometimes written as "13:00" or "13 ч."

5:00 P.M	17:00 or 17 ч.
7:30 P.M	19:30
11:00 P.M	23:00 or 23 ч.

If this system confuses you or you simply want to doublecheck, remember to subtract twelve from the numbers thirteen through twenty-four.

You can be sure to make yourself understood if you use these words:

вчера (*fchiráh*)	yesterday
сегодня (*sivóhdnya*)	today
завтра (*záhftra*)	tomorrow
утром (*óotram*)	in the morning
днём (*dnyom*)	in the afternoon
вечером (*vyéchiram*)	in the evening

Combining words from the two columns above gives you: "this afternoon" (**сегодня днём**/*sivóhdnya dnyom*), "this evening" (**сегодня вечером**/*sivóhdnya vyéchiram*), "tomorrow morning" (**завтра утром**/*záhftra óotram*), etc.

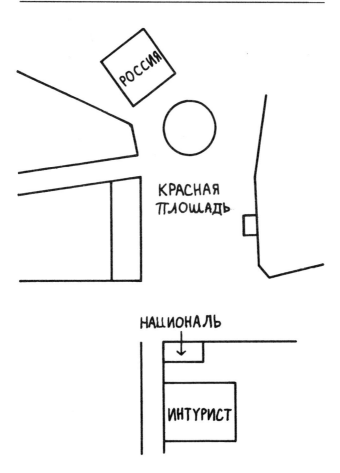

1 You are standing in front of the Intourist Hotel facing
Red Square. What are the correct instructions to get to the
following places?

    a Красная площадь (*Kráhsnaya plóhshat*)
    b гостиница «Россия» (*gastéenitsa "Rasséeya"*)
    c ресторан «Националь» (*ristaráhn "Natsianáhl"*)

2 There is quite a line at the desk where you order cars. It seems the young lady is having some trouble. She understands the time but is confused about whether the orders are for today or tomorrow, morning, afternoon, or evening. Can you help her?

   a Mrs. Johnson wants a car for six o'clock this evening.

   b Mr. and Mrs. James have to leave for the airport at eight o'clock tomorrow morning.

   c Mrs. Knight wants to go to the Ministry of Foreign Trade at two o'clock this afternoon.

   d Mr. Williams wants to drive over to the embassy at eleven o'clock this morning.

   e You need a car at one o'clock tomorrow afternoon.

3 A car and driver have been assigned to you for the whole day. Can you explain to him your schedule in Russian?

   a 8:00 Breakfast at the American embassy.

   b 9:00 Planning session at Rossiya Hotel.

   c 12:00 Lunch at the National restaurant.

   d 2:00 Negotiating session at the Ministry of Foreign Trade (Министерство Внешней Торговли /*Ministyérstva Vnyéshniy Targóhvli*)

   e 5:00 Departure for Sheremetyevo Airport.

4 Here are the names of five metro stations. Look at them closely and see if you can recognize them when you get to your stop. Библиотека им. Ленина (*Bibliatyéka éemini Lyénina*), Проспект Маркса (*Praspyékt Máhrksa*), Университетская (*Oonivirsityétskaya*), Спортивная (*Spartéevnaya*), Сокольники (*Sakóhlniki*).

   a For the soccer stadium, you ride to "Sportivnaya."

   b For the Kremlin and Palace of Congresses, take the ride to Lenin library ("Biblioteka imeni Lenina").

   c The circus is near the university.

   d The National restaurant and downtown area are near the exit "Prospekt Marksa."

   e Where do I get off for Sokolniki Park?

It's worth knowing

Arranging transportation

If you are traveling to the Soviet Union with a group, most of your transportation will be provided. If you are going alone as a tourist or on business, you can arrange for a car and driver from Intourist either before your departure or after your arrival. Normally you will make arrangements for the car and driver at the Service Bureau (**Бюро обслуживания**/*Byooróh apslóozhivaniya*) the day before you need the service.

Whether you are on your own or with a group, you should not hesitate to stroll around town. Don't be shy. Moscow, Leningrad, and the other large Soviet cities are always crowded with tourists and visitors from out of town. Since it is not always easy to find a map, they ask for directions all the time. But don't be put off by the answer **Я не знаю** (*Ya nye znáhyoo*). It means, "I don't know." Just ask the next person who comes by.

Taxis

You might want to go out by yourself in the evening—to the theater, a restaurant, or the sports arena. You can always take a taxi. These cars have a small, green light in the windshield. If the light is on, the cab is free, and you should hop right in. Many Russians like to sit alongside the driver; the view is better. There is a meter in the cab, and all you have to pay is the meter fare at the end of your trip; but a small tip of twenty to fifty kopecks will be warmly welcomed.

The metro

If you really want to launch out on your own, you might think of riding the subway or, as Russians call it, the metro (**метро**). You will need a five-kopeck coin, which can be obtained at one of the change machines near the entrance.

You simply deposit the coin in the gate, wait for the green light, and walk through. The signs in front of you will list every station that the trains go to. After you have descended the escalator, look along the wall for a layout of where you are and how many stops there are to your destination. Of course, you'll have to make out the Russian letters, but you'll know how to "get by" with the alphabet before the end of our course.

If you can't find your way, approach one of the passengers and say the name of the station of your destination. Someone will surely be willing to get you on the right train. He or she might even ride the whole way with you.

6 Getting by at the theater

Conversations

Checking your coat

Attendant	Добрый вечер. Вам нужен бинокль?
Theatergoer	**Да, пожалуйста.**
Attendant	Сколько? Один, два?
Theatergoer	**Два, пожалуйста. Сколько стоит?**
Attendant	Шестьдесят копеек. Вот ваш номерок.
Theatergoer	**Спасибо.**

Вам нужен бинокль?	Do you need opera glasses?
Вот ваш номерок.	Here is your claim check.

Buying a program

Theatergoer	**Сколько стоит программка?**
Usher	Программка стоит двенадцать копеек. Сколько вам?
Theatergoer	**Две, пожалуйста.**
Usher	Вот ваши программки. Двадцать четыре копейки.

Вот ваши программки.	Here are your programs.

Finding your seats

Usher	Ваши билеты, пожалуйста.
Theatergoer	Вот они. **Где наши места?**
Usher	Ряд семь, места пять и шесть.
Theatergoer	**Извините. Я только немного говорю по-русски. Покажите, пожалуйста.**
Usher	Я вам покажу.
Theatergoer	**Спасибо.**

Ваши билеты, пожалуйста.	Your tickets, please.
Где наши места?	Where are our seats?
Ряд семь, места пять и шесть.	Row seven, seats five and six.
Я только немного говорю по-русски.	I speak only a little Russian.

Getting something to eat

Theatergoer	**Бутерброд с сыром. Два, пожалуйста.**
Hostess	Хорошо. Два бутерброда с сыром. Что ещё?
Theatergoer	**Мороженое. Два, пожалуйста.**
Hostess	Хорошо; а ещё что-нибудь?
Theatergoer	**Шампанское. Два стакана.**
Hostess	Два стакана. Это будет пять рублей тридцать шесть копеек.

Что ещё?	What else?
Ещё что-нибудь?	Will there be anything else?
Это будет	That comes to . . . .

Language summary

What you need to say

What you want

Мне бинокль. (*Mnye binóhkl.*)	opera glasses
Мне програмка. (*Mnye pragráhmka.*)	a program
Где наши места? (*Gdye náhshi mistáh?*)	your seats

Something to eat . . .

икра (*ikráh*)	caviar
бутерброд с ветчиной (*bootirbróht s vitchinóy*)	ham sandwich

бутерброд с колбасой (*bootirbróht s kalbasóy*)	salami sandwich
бутерброд с сыром (*bootirbróht s sýram*)	cheese sandwich
мороженое (*maróhzhinayi*)	ice cream

and to drink

шампанское (*shampáhnskayi*)	champagne
вино (*vinóh*)	wine
сок (*sohk*)	juice
лимонад (*limanáht*)	soft drink

When all else fails

Я только немного говорю по-русски. (*Ya tóhlka nimnóhga gavaryóo pa-róosski.*)	I speak only a little Russian.
Покажите, пожалуйста. (*Pakazhíti, pazháhlasta.*)	Please show me.
Напишите это, пожалуйста. (*Napishíti éhta, pazháhlasta.*)	Please write it down.

What you need to listen for

Вам нужен (*Vahm nóozhin*) . . .?	Do you need . . .?
Вы хотите(*Vy khatéeti*) . . .?	Do you want . . .?
Ваши билеты, пожалуйста. (*Váhshi bilyéty, pazháhlasta.*)	Your tickets, please.
Что ещё? (*Shtoh yishóh?*)	What else?
Ещё что-нибудь? (*Yishóh shtóh-niboot?*)	Will there be anything else?

Explanations

You have already come to appreciate how Russian nouns and pronouns can change according to their function in a sentence. Adjectives and modifiers also change their endings according to the word that they go with. The one word that interests us most is the word for "your" **ваш** *(vahsh)*. Notice that it looks a little like the words **вас** *(vahs)* and **вам** *(vahm)*, which you have already learned. The basic rule is this: We say **ваш** *(vahsh)* with words that end in a consonant, **ваша** *(váhsha)* if the word ends in **a** or **я**, **ваше** *(váhshe)* if it ends in **o** or **e**, and **ваши** *(váhshi)* for all plurals.

ваш паспорт	*(vahsh páhspart)*
ваша декларация	*(váhsha diklaráhtsiya)*
ваше место	*(váhshe myésta)*
ваши билеты	*(váhshi bilyéty)*

You've already seen with prices and times that the word following the number changes form. The same thing is true of all Russian nouns. To speak correctly all of the time, you would have to learn a whole set of endings.

Here's an easy way to "get by." Just say what you want, and follow it with the appropriate phrase from below to indicate how many.

Бутерброд с сыром.	*(Bootirbróht s sýram.)*
Два, пожалуйста.	*(Dvah, pazháhlasta.)*
Мороженое.	*(Maróhzhinayi)*
Три, пожалуйста.	*(Tree, pazháhlasta.)*
Пиво.	*(Péeva.)*
Четыре, пожалуйста.	*(Chitýri, pazháhlasta.)*

When the noun is feminine (if it ends in **a** or **я**), you should say **две** for the number "two."

Програмка.	*(Pragráhmka.)*
Две, пожалуйста.	*(Dvye, pazháhlasta.)*
Книга.	*(Knéega.)*
Две, пожалуйста.	*(Dvye, pazháhlasta.)*

Exercises

1 You've been elected to get the refreshments for the group. Look at your list and see if you can satisfy everyone's desires.

three beers
four soft drinks
two glasses of champagne
four portions of caviar
six ham sandwiches

a

b

c

2 Look at the section "it's worth knowing" concerning theater tickets. Then look at the tickets and see if you can find your seats.

    a Where is Martha sitting?
    b What about Harry?
    c Where is your seat?

3 a Ваши билеты, пожалуйста.
(*Váhshi bilyéty, pazháhlasta.*)
Does she want your tickets or claim check?

b Вам програмка?
(*Vahm pragráhmka?*)
Are you being offered opera glasses or a program?

c Ваш номерок, пожалуйста.
(*Vash namiróhk, pazháhlasta.*)
Should you give her your claim check or the opera glasses?

4 There are lots of signs at the theater. It's a good opportunity to practice your reading skills. Can you find the signs meaning the following: Men's Room, Ladies' Room, Box Office (Cashier), Buffet, Balcony?

a Буфет (*Boofýet*)
b Касса (*Káhssa*)
c Мужской туалет (*Mooshskóy tooalyét*)
d Балкон (*Balkóhn*)
e Женский туалет (*Zhénskiy tooalyét*)

It's worth knowing

Checking your coats

When you enter the theater, an usher will tear off part of your ticket stub. You should then go to check your coats and hats. It is impolite not to check your things. Russians are very proud of their theaters; many of them are architectural masterpieces, both inside and out.

The service is free and tips are not accepted. But you will probably be offered opera glasses (**бинокль**/*binóhkl*), which are the private property of these attendants; by renting them you help supplement their wages. The rental fee is modest—between twenty and fifty kopecks. So why not take them—you might even get used to them. There is another good reason to take the glasses. A custom universally observed is that those with **бинокль** go immediately to the head of the line to retrieve their garments after the performance. The time saved is more than worth the very minor cost of the service.

The program

Before you enter the hall, try to purchase a program. They are inexpensive, make great mementos of your visit, and you will even be able to read the names of the performers when you have completed your course.

Your ticket

Your row (**ряд**/*ryat*) and seat (**место**/*myésta*) will be clearly indicated on your ticket, but don't be afraid to ask for assistance if you can't keep track of where you are. Check to see if you are in the middle (**середина**/ *siridéena*), on the right side (**правая сторона**/*práhvaya staranáh*), or left (**левая сторона**/*lyévay staranáh*). Are you in the orchestra or the balcony?

Here are the most common listings:

партер (*partyér*)	orchestra
амфитеатр (*amfitiáhtr*)	amphitheater
белэтаж (*byeletáhsh*)	dress circle
балкон (*balkóhn*)	balcony
первый ярус (*pyérviy yároos*)	first ring
второй ярус (*ftaróy yároos*)	second ring

The buffet

Since most Russians come to the theater directly from work, they use the buffet for a light dinner. This can range from champagne (**шампанское**/*shampáhnskayi*) and caviar (**икра**/*ikráh*) at the more elegant theaters to simple open-faced sandwiches (**бутерброд**/*bootirbróht*) with cheese (**с сыром**/*s sýram*), salami (**с колбасой**/ *s kalbasóy*), or ham (**с ветчиной**/*s vitchinóy*).

The most sumptuous of buffets is the one located in the Grand Hall of the Palace of Congresses (**Дворец съездов**/ *Dvaryéts syézdaf*).

Moscow theaters

All of us have heard of the Bolshoi Theater (**Большой театр**/*Balshóy tiáhtr*), but you might also catch the artists of the Bolshoi doing a performance in the Palace of Congresses. An often-overlooked theater that is certainly worth a visit is the Stanislavsky Musical Theater. Ask your guide or someone in the Service Bureau (**Бюро обслуживания**/*Byooróh apslóozhivahniya*) to call ahead. If you are really adventuresome, go yourself to see the manager (**администратор**/*administráhtar*) before the performance. If you tell him that you're an American (**Я американец**/*Ya amirikáhnits*) and that you really want to see his theater, maybe he'll let you have a couple of the seats that are always held in reserve until the last minute.

Reference section

Pronunciation guide

А	а	a, as in "father"
Б	б	b
В	в	v
Г	г	g, as in "go"
Д	д	d
Е	е	ye
Ё	ё	yo
Ж	ж	s, as in "measure"
З	з	z, as in "zoo"
И	и	ee, as in "bee"
Й	й	y, as in "boy"
К	к	k
Л	л	l
М	м	m
Н	н	n
О	о	o
П	п	p
Р	р	r
С	с	s, as in "sit"
Т	т	t
У	у	oo, as in "hoot"
Ф	ф	f
Х	х	ch, as in "Bach"
Ц	ц	ts, as in "tsar"
Ч	ч	ch, as in "cheap"
Ш	ш	sh, as in "shoe"
Щ	щ	sh, as in "sheet"
Ъ	ъ	hard sign
Ы	ы	i, as in "visual"
Ь	ь	soft sign
Э	э	e, as in "bet"
Ю	ю	you
Я	я	ya

Numbers

0	нуль	(*nool*)
1	один	(*adéen*)
2	два	(*dvah*)
3	три	(*tree*)
4	четыре	(*chitýri*)
5	пять	(*pyat*)
6	шесть	(*shest*)
7	семь	(*syem*)
8	восемь	(*vóhsim*)
9	девять	(*dyévit*)
10	десять	(*dyésit*)
11	одиннадцать	(*adéenatsat*)
12	двенадцать	(*dvináhtsat*)
13	тринадцать	(*trináhtsat*)
14	четырнадцать	(*chitýrnatsat*)
15	пятнадцать	(*pitnáhtsat*)
16	шестнадцать	(*shisnáhtsat*)
17	семнадцать	(*simnáhtsat*)
18	восемнадцать	(*vasimnáhtsat*)
19	девятнадцать	(*divitnáhtsat*)
20	двадцать	(*dváhtsat*)
21	двадцать один	(*dváhtsat adéen*)
22	двадцать два	(*dváhtsat dvah*)
23	двадцать три	(*dváhtsat tree*)
24	двадцать четыре	(*dváhtsat chitýri*)
25	двадцать пять	(*dváhtsat pyat*)
26	двадцать шесть	(*dváhtsat shest*)
27	двадцать семь	(*dváhtsat syem*)
28	двадцать восемь	(*dváhtsat vóhsim*)
29	двадцать девять	(*dváhtsat dyévit*)
30	тридцать	(*tréetsat*)
40	сорок	(*sóhrak*)
50	пятьдесят	(*pitdisyát*)
60	шестьдесят	(*shisdisyát*)
70	семьдесят	(*syémdisit*)
80	восемьдесят	(*vóhsimdisit*)
90	девяносто	(*divinóhsta*)
100	сто	(*stoh*)

Prices

1 ruble	один рубль (*adéen roobl*)
2 rubles	два рубля (*dvah rooblyá*)
3 rubles	три рубля (*tree rooblyá*)
4 rubles	четыре рубля (*chitýri rooblyá*)
5 rubles	пять рублей (*pyat rooblyéy*)
6 rubles	шесть рублей (*shest rooblyéy*)
21 rubles	двадцать один рубль (*dváhtsat adéen roobl*)
22 rubles	двадцать два рубля (*dváhtsat dvah rooblyá*)
25 rubles	двадцать пять рублей (*dváhtsat pyat rooblyéy*)

1 kopeck	одна копейка (*adnáh kapyéyka*)
2 kopecks	две копейки (*dvye kapyéyki*)
3 kopecks	три копейки (*tree kapyéyki*)
4 kopecks	четыре копейки (*chitýri kapyéyki*)
5 kopecks	пять копеек (*pyat kapyéik*)
6 kopecks	шесть копеек (*shest kapyéik*)
21 kopecks	двадцать одна копейка (*dváhtsat adnáh kapyéyka*)
22 kopecks	двадцать две копейки (*dváhtsat dvye kapyéyki*)
25 kopecks	двадцать пять копеек (*dváhtsat pyat kapyéik*)

Time

1:00	(один) час (*adéen chahs*)
2:00	два часа (*dvah chasáh*)
3:00	три часа (*tree chasáh*)
4:00	четыре часа (*chitýri chasáh*)
5:00	пять часов (*pyat chasóhf*)
6:00	шесть часов (*shest chasóhf*)
7:00	семь часов (*syem chasóhf*)
8:00	восемь часов (*vóhsim chasóhf*)
9:00	девять часов (*dyévit chasóhf*)
10:00	десять часов (*dyésit chasóhf*)
11:00	одиннадцать часов (*adéenatsat chasóhf*)
12:00	двенадцать часов (*dvináhtsat chasóhf*)

Days of the week

Sunday	воскресенье (*vaskrisyényi*)
Monday	понедельник (*panidyélnik*)
Tuesday	вторник (*ftóhrnik*)
Wednesday	среда (*sridá*)
Thursday	четверг (*chitvyérk*)
Friday	пятница (*pyátnitsa*)
Saturday	суббота (*soobóhta*)

Months of the year

January	январь (*yanváhr*)
February	февраль (*fivráhl*)
March	март (*mahrt*)
April	апрель (*aprýel*)
May	май (*may*)
June	июнь (*iyóon*)
July	июль (*iyóol*)
August	август (*áhvgoost*)
September	сентябрь (*sintyábr*)
October	октябрь (*aktyábr*)
November	ноябрь (*nayábr*)
December	декабрь (*dikábr*)

Answers to exercises

Урок номер два. (*Ooróhk nóhmir dvah.*)

1 **a** Да, пожалуйста. (*Dah, pazháhlasta.*)
  b Нет, спасибо. (*Nyet, spaséeba.*)
  c Нет, спасибо. (*Nyet, spaséeba.*)

2 **b, c, c.**

3 **a** Здравствуйте. Кофе, пожалуйста.
    (*Zdráhstvuyti. Kóhfi, pazháhlasta.*)
  b Девушка. Водка с соком и коньяк.
    (*Dyévooshka. Vóhtka s sóhkam, pazháhlasta.*)
  c Добрый вечер. У вас есть пиво? Два,
    пожалуйста. (*Dóhbriy vyéchir. Oo vahs yest
    péeva? Dvah, pazháhlasta.*)

4 **a** Белое сухое вино, пожалуйста. (*Byélayi
    sookhóhyi vinóh, pazháhlasta.*)
  b Ещё джин с тоником. (*Yishóh dzhin s tóhnikam.*)
  c Молодой человек. Сколько с меня? (*Maladóy
    chilavyék. Skóhlka s minyá?*)

5 2+1=3 три (*tree*)
   6+3=9 девять (*dyévit*)
   8−7=1 один (*adéen*)
   10−4=6 шесть (*shest*)
   9−5=4 четыре (*chitýri*)

Урок номер три. (*Ooróhk nóhmir tree.*)

1 **a** Mr. Richards.
  b Room 19.
  c Third floor.

2 **a** Семнадцать, пожалуйста. (*Simnáhtsat,
    pazháhlasta.*)
  b Пять, пожалуйста. (*Pyat, pazháhlasta.*)
  c Двенадцать, пожалуйста. (*Dvináhtsat,
    pazháhlasta.*)

3 **b** Доллары. (*Dóhllary.*)
   b Your customs declaration.
   a Sign the receipt.

4 **a** Сок, пожалуйста. (*Sohk, pazháhlasta.*)
   b Яичница, пожалуйста. (*Yaéechnitsa, pazháhlasta.*)
   c Чай, пожалуйста. (*Chay, pazháhlasta.*)

5 **a** The bank is on the fourth floor.
   b The buffet is on the seventh floor.
   c The men's room is on the second floor.
   d The restaurant is on the eleventh floor.
   e Your room is on the sixth floor.

Урок номер четыре. (*Ooróhk nóhmir chitýri.*)

1 **a** 3 р. 25 к.   **b** 45 к.
   c 1 р. 13 к.   **d** 6 р. 48 к.
   e 87 к.

2 **a** 3 р.   **b** 10 р. 20 к.
   c 60 к.   **d** 1 р. 50 к.
   e 8 р. 90 к.

3 **a** У вас есть открытки? (*Oo vahs yest atkrýtki?*)
   b Дайте мне открытки, пожалуйста. У вас есть марки? (*Dayti mnye atkrýtki, pazháhlasta. Oo vahs yest máhrki?*)
   c Сколько стоит книга? (*Skóhlka stóhit knéega?*)
   d У вас есть сигареты? Сколько стоят сигареты? (*Oo vahs yest sigaryéty? Skóhlka stóhit sigaryéty?*)

4
postcard	15 к.
stamps for postcard	35 к.
airmail envelope	47 к.
book	1 р. 30 к.
total	2 р. 27 к.

Урок номер пять. (*Ooróhk nóhmir pyat.*)

1 **a** Идите прямо. (*Idéeti pryáma.*)
   b Идите прямо, а потом налево. (*Idéeti pryáma, ah patóhm nalyéva.*)
   c Идите прямо, а потом направо. (*Idéeti pryáma, ah patóhm napráhva.*)

2 **a** Сегодня вечером. (*Sivóhdnya vyéchiram.*)
   b Завтра утром. (*Záhftra óotram.*)
   c Сегодня днём. (*Sivóhdnya dnyom.*)
   d Сегодня утром. (*Sivóhdnya óotram.*)
   e Завтра днём. (*Záhftra dnyom.*)

3 **a** В восемь часов, в американское посольство. (*V vóhsim chasóhf, v amirikáhnskayi pasóhlstva.*)
   b В девять часов, в гостиницу «Россия» (*V dyévit chasóhf, v gastéenitsoo "Rasséeya."*)
   c В двенадцать часов, в ресторан «Националь». (*V dvináhtsat chasóhf, v ristaráhn "Natsianáhl."*)
   d В два часа, в Министерство Внешней Торговли. (*V dvah chasáh, v Ministyérstva Vnyéshniy Targóhvli."*)
   e В пять часов, в аэропорт «Шереметьево. (*F pyat chasóf, v airapóhrt "Shirimyétiva."*)

4 **a** Спортивная (*Spartéevnaya*).
   b Библиотека им. Ленина (*Bibliatyéka éemini Lyénina*).
   c Университетская (*Oonivirsityétskaya*).
   d Проспект Маркса (*Praspyékt Máhrksa*).
   e Сокольники (*Sakóhlniki*).

Урок номер шесть. (*Ooróhk nóhmir shest.*)

1 Пиво. Три, пожалуйста. (*Péeva. Tree, pazháhlasta.*)
   Лимонад. Четыре, пожалуйста. (*Limanáht. Chitýri, pazháhlasta.*)

Шампанское. Два стакана, пожалуйста.
(*Shampáhnskayi. Dvah stakáhna, pazháhlasta.*)
Икра. Четыре, пожалуйста.
(*Ikráh, Chitýri, pazháhlasta.*)
Бутерброд с ветчиной. Шесть, пожалуйста.
(*Bootirbróht s vitchinóy. Shest, pazháhlasta.*)

2   **a**   Balcony, right side; row 5, seat 84.
    b   Amphitheater, center; row 40, seat 19.
    c   Orchestra, left side; row 14, seat 54.

3   **a**   Tickets.
    b   Program.
    c   Claim check.

4   **a**   Buffet.
    b   Box Office.
    c   Men's Room.
    d   Balcony.
    e   Ladies' Room.

Russian Travel Bureau
20 East 46th Street
New York, N.Y. 10017
(212) 986-1500
(800) 847-1800

Citizen Exchange
    Council, Inc.
18 East 41st Street
New York, N.Y. 10017
(212) 889-7960

Soviet Consulate
1825 Phelps Place N.W.
Washington, D.C. 20008
(202) 332-1482
(202) 332-1483

American Embassy
Ulitsa Chaikovskogo 19/21
Moscow
252-2451 through 252-2459

British Consulate
Naberezhnaya
Morisa Toreza 14
Moscow
241-1035

Australian Embassy
13 Kropotkinsky Pereulok
Moscow
246-5011

American Express Company
21-A Sadovo-Kudrinskaya
Moscow
254-4305
254-4505

Chase Manhattan Bank
World Trade Center
Krasnopresnenskaya
    Naberezhnaya 12
Moscow
253-8354

Lloyd's Bank International
World Trade Center
Krasnopresnenskaya
    Naberezhnaya 12
Room 1808
Moscow
230-2720

Russian–English word list

The English meanings apply to the words as they are used in this book.

In words of more than one syllable, stress is indicated by an accent mark (´).

Plural forms that you are likely to need are given immediately following the singular forms.

А

а (*ah*) and, but

áвгуст (*áhvgoost*) August

авиаписьмó, авиапи́сьма (*aviapismóh, aviapéesma*) airmail letter(s)

администрáтор (*administráhtar*) manager

Амéрика (*Amyérika*) America

америкáнец (*amirikáhnits*) American (male)

америкáнка (*amirikáhnka*) American (female)

америкáнское, америкáнские (*amirikáhnskayi, amirikáhnskiyi*) American (*adj.*)

амфитеáтр (*amfitiáhtr*) amphitheater

апрéль (*apryél*) April

аэропóрт (*airapóhrt*) airport

Аэрофлóт (*airaflóht*) Aeroflot

Б

балкóн (*balkóhn*) balcony

банк (*bahnk*) bank

бар (*bahr*) bar

бéлое (*byélayi*) white

белэтáж (*byeletáhsh*) dress circle

Берёзка (*Biryóska*) Beriozka store

Библиотéка им. Лéнина (*Bibliatyéka éemini Lyénina*)) Lenin library

билéт, билéты (*bilyét, bilyéty*) ticket(s)

Б (continued)

бинóкль (*binóhkl*) opera glasses

блок, блóки (*blohk, blóhki*) carton(s) of cigarettes

большóе (*balshóhyi*) big

Большóе спаси́бо. (*Balshóhyi spaséeba.*) Thank you very much.

Большóй теáтр (*Balshóy tiáhtr*) Bolshoi Theater

бýдет, бýдете (*bóodit, bóoditi*) (he, she) will, (you) will

бутербрóд, бутербрóды (*bootirbróht, bootirbróhdy*) sandwich(es)

буфéт (*boofyét*) buffet, coffee shop

бюрó (*byooróh*) bureau

Бюрó обслýживания (*byooróh apslóozhivaniya*) Service Bureau

В

в (*v*) in, to, at

валю́та (*valyóota*) foreign currency

ваш, вáша, вáше, вáши (*vahsh, váhsha, váhshe, váhshi*) your

ветчинá (*vitchináh*) ham

с ветчинóй (*s vitchinóy*) with ham

вéчером (*vyéchiram*) (in the) evening

винó (*vinóh*) wine

Ви́нстон (*Véenstan*) Winston

во́дка (*vóhtka*) vodka

во́дка с со́ком (*vóhtka s sókham*) screwdriver (vodka with juice)

Возьми́те. (*Vazméeti.*) Take!

Я возьму́. (*Ya vazmóo.*) I'll take.

вон там (*vohn tahm*) over there

восемна́дцать (*vasimnáhtsat*) eighteen

во́семь (*vóhsim*) eight

во́семьдесят (*vóhsimdisit*) eighty

воскресе́нье (*vaskrisyényi*) Sunday

восьмо́й (*vasmóy*) eighth

вот (*voht*) here (it) is

На како́е вре́мя? (*Na kakóhye vryémya?*) For what time?

вто́рник (*ftóhrnik*) Tuesday

второ́й (*ftaróy*) second

вчера́ (*fchiráh*) yesterday

вход (*fkhóht*) entrance

вы, вас, вам (*vy, vahs, vahm*) you

Вы́пишите. (*Výpishiti.*) Write out!

вы́ход (*výkhat*) exit

Г

газе́та, газе́ты (*gazyéta, gazyéty*) newspaper(s)

гардеро́б (*gardiróhp*) cloakroom

где (*gdye*) where

Я говорю́ по-ру́сски. (*Ya gavaryóo pa-róosski.*) I speak Russian.

гости́ница (*gastéenitsa*) hotel

Д

да (*dah*) yes

Да́йте. (*Dáyti.*) Give!

два, две (*dvah, dvye*) two

два́дцать (*dváhtsat*) twenty

двена́дцать (*dvináhtsat*) twelve

двена́дцатый (*dvináhtsatiy*) twelfth

Дворе́ц съе́здов (*Dvaryéts syézdaf*) Palace of Congresses

Де́вушка. (*Dyévooshka.*) Miss!

девятна́дцать (*divitnáhtsat*) nineteen

де́вять (*dyévit*) nine

девя́тый (*divyátiy*) ninth

дежу́рная (*dizhóornaya*) attendant (female)

дека́брь (*dikáhbr*) December

деклара́ция (*diklaráhtsiya*) declaration

де́сять (*dyésit*) ten

деся́тый (*disyátiy*) tenth

джин (*dzhin*) gin

джин с то́ником (*dzhin s tóhnikam*) gin and tonic

днём (*dnyom*) (in the) afternoon

До́брый ве́чер. (*Dóhbriy vyéchir.*) Good evening.

До́брый день. (*Dóhbriy dyen.*) Good afternoon.

До́брое у́тро. (*Dóhbrayi óotra.*) Good morning.

до́ллар, до́ллары (*dóhllar, dóhllary*) dollar(s)

До свида́ния. (*Da svidáhniya.*) Good-bye.

Е

есть (*yest*) have

У вас есть? (*Oo vahs yest?*) Do you have?

У нас есть. (*Oo nahs yest.*) We have it.

У нас нет. (*Oo nahs nyet.*) We don't have it.

У меня́ есть. (*Oo minyá yest.*) I have it.

е́хать (*yékhat*) ride

ещё (*yishóh*) another

Ещё раз. (*Yishóh ras.*) One more time.

Что ещё? (*Shtoh yishóh?*) What else?

Ещё что-нибу́дь? (*Yishóh shtóh-niboot?*) Anything else?

Ж

ждать (*zhdat*) wait

жéнский (*zhénskiy*) female (*adj.*)

жéнский туалéт (*zhénskiy tooalyét*) ladies' room

журнáл, журнáлы (*zhoornáhl, zhoornáhly*) magazine(s)

З

Не забýдьте. (*Nye zabóoti.*) Don't forget.

завернýть (*zavirnóot*) wrap (*v.*)

   Вам завернýть? (*Vahm zavirnóot?*) Should I wrap it for you?

зáвтра (*záhftra*) tomorrow

заказáть (*zakazáht*) order (*v.*)

зал (*zahl*) hall, conference room

здесь (*zdyes*) here

Здрáвствуйте. (*Zdráhstvuyti.*) Hello.

знать (*znat*) know

   Я знáю. (*Ya znáhyoo*) I know.

   Вы не знáете? (*Vy nye znáhiti?*) Do you happen to know?

   Как вас зовýт? (*Kahk vahs zavóot?*) What is your name?

   Меня зовýт (*Minyá zavóot*).... My name is. . . .

И

и (*ee*) and

Идúте. (*Idéeti.*) Go!

Извинúте. (*Izvinéeti.*) Excuse me.

икрá (*ikráh*) caviar

úли (*éeli*) or

Интурúст (*Intooréest*) Intourist

úюль (*iyóol*) July

úюнь (*iyóon*) June

К

как (*kahk*) how

Как вас зовýт? (*Kahk vahs zavóot?*) What's your name?

Какýю? (*Kakóoyoo?*) Which one?

кáрточка, кáрточки (*káhrtachka, káhrtachki*) card(s)

кáсса (*káhssa*) cashier

кафé (*kafyé*) café

квитáнция (*kvitáhntsiya*) receipt

Кент (*Kyent*) Kent

кефúр (*kiféer*) kefir, yogurt

киóск (*kióhsk*) kiosk

ключ, ключú (*klyooch, klyoochée*) key(s)

кнúга, кнúги (*knéega, knéegi*) book(s)

когдá (*kagdáh*) when

колбасá (*kalbasáh*) salami

   с колбасóй (*s kalbasóy*) with salami

конвéрт, конвéрты (*kanvyért, kanvyérty*) envelope(s)

коньяк (*kanyák*) cognac

копéйка, копéйки (*kapyéyka, kapyéyki*) kopeck(s)

кóфе (*kóhfi*) coffee

Крáсная плóщадь (*Kráhsnaya plóhshat*) Red Square

крáсное (*kráhsnayi*) red

к сожалéнию (*k sazhalyéniyoo*) unfortunately

Кудá? (*Koodáh?*) Where to?

курúть (*kooréet*) smoke

Л

лéвая сторонá (*lyévaya staranáh*) left side

Лéнин (*Lyénin*) Lenin

лимонáд (*limanáht*) soft drink

лифт (*leeft*) elevator

М

май (*may*) May

мáрка, мáрки (*máhrka, máhrki*) German mark(s)

ма́рка, ма́рки (*máhrka, máhrki*) stamp(s)

Ма́рлборо (*Máhrlbara*) Marlboro

март (*mahrt*) March

ма́сло (*máhsla*) butter

маши́на, маши́ны (*mashína, mashíny*) car(s)

ме́дленнее (*myédliniyi*) slower

ме́сто, места́ (*myésta, mistáh*) place(s), seat(s)

метро́ (*mitróh*) metro, subway

минера́льная вода́ (*miniráhlnaya vadáh*) mineral water

Министе́рство Вне́шней Торго́вли (*Ministyérstva Vnyéshniy Targóhvli*) Ministry of Foreign Trade

Ми́стер (*Méestir*) Mister

мне (*mnye*) me

Мо́жно? (*Móhzhna?*) Can one? May I?

мой (*moy*) my

молодо́й челове́к (*maladóy chilavyék*) young man

молоко́ (*malakóh*) milk

с молоко́м (*s malakóhm*) with milk

моро́женое (*maróhzhinayi*) ice cream

Москва́ (*Maskváh*) Moscow

мужско́й (*mooshskóy*) male (*adj.*)

мужско́й туале́т (*mooshskóy tooalyét*) men's room

Н

на (*nah*) to, on, for

нале́во (*nalyéva*) to the left

Напиши́те. (*Napishíti.*) Write it down.

напра́во (*napráhva*) to the right

нахо́дится (*nakhóhditsa*) (is) located

«Национа́ль» (*Natsianáhl*) National (hotel)

нача́ло (*nacháhla*) beginning

на́ши (*náhshi*) our

немно́го (*nimnóhga*) (a) little

Не э́ту, а ту. (*Nye éhtoo, ah too.*) Not this one; that one.

нет (*nyet*) no

но́мер (*nóhmir*) room number

номеро́к (*namiróhk*) claim check

ноя́брь (*nayábr*) November

ну́жен, нужна́, ну́жно (*nóozhin, noozhnáh, nóozhna*) need, have to

О

обменя́ть (*abminyát*) exchange

оди́н (*adéen*) one

оди́ннадцать (*adéenatsat*) eleven

оди́ннадцатый (*adéenatsatiy*) eleventh

октя́брь (*aktyábr*) October

они́ (*anée*) they

оно́ (*anóh*) it

отде́л (*atdyél*) department

откры́тка, откры́тки (*atkrýtka, atkrýtki*) postcard(s)

П

парк (*pahrk*) park

парте́р (*partyér*) orchestra

па́спорт, паспорта́ (*páhspart, paspartáh*) passport(s)

пе́рвый (*pyérviy*) first

пи́во (*péeva*) beer

плати́ть (*platéet*) pay

Плати́те. (*Platéeti.*) Pay!

Повтори́те. (*Paftaréeti.*) Repeat!

пожа́луйста (*pazháhlasta*) please, you're welcome

Покажи́те. (*Pakazhíti.*) Show! Я покажу́. (*Ya pakazhóo.*) I'll show you.

полусухо́е (*paloosookhóhyi*) semidry

помо́чь (*pamóhch*) help

понедéльник (*panidyélnik*)
Monday
попáсть (*papáhst*)   get to
по-рýсски (*pa-róosski*)
Russian
послáть (*pasláht*)   send
Посмотрúте. (*Pasmatréeti.*)
Look!
посóльство (*pasóhlstva*)
embassy
америкáнское посóльство
(*amirikáhnskayi pasóhlstva*)
American embassy
потóм (*patóhm*)   then
пóчта (*póhchta*)   post office
прáвая сторонá (*práhvaya
staranáh*)   right side
Я принесý. (*Ya prinisóo.*)
I'll bring it.
Приходúте. (*Prikhadéeti.*)
Come!
прогрáмка, прогрáмки
(*pragráhmka, pragráhmki*)
theater program(s)
проéхать (*prayékhat*)   get to
(by vehicle)
пройтú (*praytée*)   get to (on
foot)
прóпуск, прóпуски
(*próhpoosk, próhpooski*)
pass(es) (*n.*)
проспéкт Мáркса (*praspyékt
Máhrksa*)   Marx Prospect
прямо (*pryáma*)   straight ahead
пятница (*pyátnitsa*)   Friday
пятнáдцать (*pitnáhtsat*)
fifteen
пять (*pyat*)   five
пятый (*pyátiy*)   fifth
пятьдесят (*pitdisyát*)   fifty

Р

Распишúтесь. (*Raspishítis.*)
Sign!
ресторáн (*ristaráhn*)
restaurant
«Россúя» (*Rasséeya*)   Rossiya
(hotel)

рубль, рублú (*roobl, rooblée*)
ruble(s)
ряд (*ryat*)   row

С

сáхар (*sáhkar*)   sugar
с сáхаром (*s sáhkharam*)
with sugar
без сáхара (*byez sáhkhara*)
without sugar
сдáча (*zdáhcha*)   change (*n.*)
сегóдня (*sivóhdnya*)   today
седьмóй (*sidmóy*)   seventh
сейчáс (*siycháhs*)   right away
семнáдцать (*simnáhtsat*)
seventeen
семь (*syem*)   seven
сéмьдесят (*syémdisit*)   seventy
сентябрь (*sintyábr*)   September
серединá (*siridéena*)   center
сигарéта, сигарéты (*sigaryéta,
sigaryéty*)   cigarette(s)
Скажúте. (*Skazhíti.*)   Tell me!
скóлько (*skóhlka*)   how much
Скóлько с меня? (*Skóhlka s
minyá?*)   How much do I owe?
сок, сóки (*sohk, sóhki*)
juice(s)
Сокóльники (*Sakóhlniki*)
Sokolniki
сóрок (*sóhrak*)   forty
сосúска, сосúски (*saséeska,
saséeski*)   hot dog(s)
спасúбо (*spaséeba*)   thank you
спасúбо большóе (*spaséeba
balshóhyi*)   thank you very
much
Спортúвная (*Spartéevnaya*)
Sportivnaya (station)
срáзу (*sráhzoo*)   immediately
средá (*sridáh*)   Wednesday
стакáн, стакáны (*stakháhn,
stakháhny*)   glass(es)
стáнция (*stáhntsiya*)   station
До какóй стáнции? (*Da
kakóy stántsii?*)   To which
station?
стó (*stoh*)   hundred

стóит, стóят (*stóhit, stóhit*)
costs, cost
Скóлько стóит? (*Skóhlka stóhit?*) How much does it cost?
Стóйте. (*Stóyti.*) Wait!
суббóта (*soobbóhta*) Saturday
сувенир, сувениры (*soovinéer, soovinéery*) souvenir(s)
сухóе (*sookhóhyi*) dry
сыр (*syr*) cheese
с сыром (*s sýram*) with cheese

Т

такси (*taksée*) taxi
там (*tahm*) there
теáтр (*tiáhtr*) theater
телефóн (*tilifóhn*) telephone
тогдá (*tagdáh*) then
тóлько (*tóhlka*) only
тóник (*tóhnik*) tonic
трéтий (*tryétiy*) third
три (*tree*) three
тридцать (*tréetsat*) thirty
тринáдцать (*trináhtsat*) thirteen
туалéт, туалéты (*tooalyét, tooalyéty*) restroom(s)
тудá (*toodáh*) (to) there

У

Увидите. (*Oovéediti.*) You'll see.
Университéтская (*Oonivirsityétskaya*) University (station)
урóк (*ooróhk*) lesson
ýтром (*óotram*) (in the) morning

Х

хлеб (*khlyep*) bread
я хочý (*ya khachóo*) I want
Вы хотите? (*Vy khatéeti?*) Do you want?
хорóшее (*kharóhshiyi*) good
хорошó (*kharashóh*) OK

Ф

феврáль (*fivrahl*) February
франк, фрáнки (*fráhnk, fráhnki*) French franc
фунт, фýнты (*foont, fóonty*) English pound

Ц

ценá (*tsináh*) price
центр (*tsentr*) center of town, downtown
цирк (*tsirk*) circus

Ч

чай (*chay*) tea
час (*chahs*) o'clock
чáшка, чáшки (*cháhshka, cháhshki*) cup(s)
чек (*chyek*) receipt
Чем вам помóчь? (*Chyem vahm pamóhch?*) How can I help you?
четвéрг (*chitvyérk*) Thursday
четвёртый (*chitvyórtiy*) fourth
четыре (*chitýri*) four
четырнадцать (*chitýrnatsat*) fourteen
что (*shtoh*) what

Ш

шампáнское (*shampáhnskayi*) champagne
швéдский стол (*shvyétskiy stohl*) smorgasbord
Шеремéтьево (*Shirimyétiva*) Sheremetyevo (airport)
шестнáдцать (*shisnáhtsat*) sixteen
шестóй (*shistóy*) sixth
шесть (*shest*) six
шестьдесят (*shisdisyát*) sixty

Э

этáж (*etáhzh*) floor
На какóм этажé? (*Na kakóhm etazhé?*) On which floor?
э́то (*éhta*) this

Я

я (*ya*)   I

яи́чница (*yaéechnitsa*)   fried
  eggs

яйцо́, я́йца (*yaytsóh, yáytsa*)
  egg(s)

янва́рь (*yanváhr*)   January

я́рус (*yároos*)   theater ring
  пе́рвый я́рус (*pyérviy
  yároos*)   first ring
  второ́й я́рус (*ftaróy yároos*)
  second ring

English-Russian word list

A

Aeroflot   Аэрофло́т
(in the) afternoon   днём
airmail letter   авиаписьмо́,
  авиапи́сьма (pl.)
airport   аэропо́рт
America   Аме́рика
American
  (adj.)   америка́нское,
  америка́нские (pl.)
  I'm an American   Я
  америка́нец (m.)   Я
  америка́нка (f.)
amphitheater   амфитеа́тр
and   и, а
another   ещё
Anything else?   Ещё
  что́-нибудь?
April   апре́ль
(we've) arrived   прие́хали
at   в
attendant   дежу́рная (f.)
August   а́вгуст

B

balcony   балко́н
bank   банк
bar   бар
beer   пи́во
beginning   нача́ло
Beriozka   Берёзка
big   большо́й
Bolshoi Theater   Большо́й
  теа́тр
book   кни́га, кни́ги (pl.)
bread   хлеб
bring
  I'll bring   я принесу́
buffet   буфе́т
bureau   бюро́
but   а
butter   ма́сло

C

cafe   кафе́
can one   мо́жно
car   маши́на, маши́ны (pl.)

card   ка́рточка, ка́рточки
  (pl.)
carton (of cigarettes)   бло́к,
  бло́ки (pl.)
cashier   ка́сса
caviar   икра́
center (in theater)   середи́на
center of town   центр
champagne   шампа́нское
change (n.)   сда́ча
cheese   сыр
  with cheese   с сы́ром
cigarette   сигаре́та
  American cigarettes
  америка́нские сигаре́ты
circus   цирк
claim check   номеро́к
cloakroom   гардеро́б
coffee   ко́фе
coffee shop   буфе́т
cognac   конья́к
Come!   Приходи́те.
cost   сто́ит, сто́ят (pl.)
  How much does it cost?
  Ско́лько сто́ит?
cup   ча́шка, ча́шки (pl.)

D

December   дека́брь
declaration   деклара́ция
department   отде́л
dollar   до́ллар, до́ллары (pl.)
downtown   центр
dress circle   белэта́ж
dry   сухо́е

E

egg   яйцо́, я́йца (pl.)
eight   во́семь
eighteen   восемна́дцать
eighth   восьмо́й
eighty   во́семьдесят
elevator   лифт
eleven   оди́ннадцать
eleventh   оди́ннадцатый

embassy посо́льство
  American embassy
  америка́нское посо́льство
entrance вход
envelope конве́рт, конве́рты
  (pl.)
(in the) evening ве́чером
exchange обменя́ть
excuse me извини́те
exit вы́ход

F
February февра́ль
female *(adj.)* же́нский
fifteen пятна́дцать
fifth пя́тый
fifty пятьдеся́т
first пе́рвый
five пять
floor эта́ж
  on which floor? на како́м
  этаже́?
for на
foreign currency валю́та
forget
  Don't forget! Не забу́дьте.
forty со́рок
four четы́ре
fourteen четы́рнадцать
fourth четвёртый
franc франк, фра́нки *(pl.)*
Friday пя́тница
fried eggs яи́чница

G
get to пройти́, прое́хать,
  попа́сть
  How can I get to? Как
  пройти́? Как прое́хать?
gin джин
  gin and tonic джин с
  то́ником
Give! Да́йте.
glass стака́н, стака́ны *(pl.)*
Go! Иди́те.
good хоро́шее
Good afternoon. До́брый
  день.

H
hall зал
ham ветчина́
  with ham с ветчино́й
have есть
  Do you have? У вас есть?
Hello. Здра́вствуйте.
help помо́чь
here здесь
here (it) is вот
hot dog соси́ска, соси́ски
  (pl.)
hotel гости́ница
how как
How much? Ско́лько?
  How much do I
  owe? Ско́лько с меня́?
hundred сто

I
I я
ice cream моро́женое
immediately сра́зу
in в
Intourist Интури́ст
it оно́

J
January янва́рь
juice со́к, со́ки *(pl.)*
July ию́ль
June ию́нь

K
kefir (yogurt) кефи́р
Kent Кент
key ключ, ключи́ *(pl.)*
kiosk кио́ск
know
  I don't know. Я не зна́ю.
  Do you happen to know? Вы
  не зна́ете?
kopeck копе́йка, копе́йки
  (pl.)

Good evening. До́брый
  ве́чер.
Good morning. До́брое у́тро.
Good-bye. До свида́ния.

L

ladies' room   же́нский туале́т

left
    left side   ле́вая сторона́
    to the left   нале́во
Lenin   Ле́нин
Lenin library   Библиоте́ка им.
    Ле́нина
lesson   уро́к
(a) little   немно́го
(is) located   нахо́дится
Look!   Посмотри́те.

M

magazine   журна́л, журна́лы
    (pl.)
male (adj.)   мужско́й
manager   администра́тор
March   март
(German) mark   ма́рка, ма́рки
    (pl.)
Marlboro   Ма́рлборо
Marx Prospect   проспе́кт
    Ма́ркса
May   май
me   мне
men's room   мужско́й туале́т
metro   метро́
milk   молоко́
    with milk   с молоко́м
mineral water   минера́льная
    вода́
Ministry of Foreign
    Trade   Министе́рство
    Вне́шней Торго́вли
Miss!   Де́вушка.
Mister   Ми́стер
Monday   понеде́льник
(in the) morning   у́тром
Moscow   Москва́
my   мой (m.)

N

name
    What's your name?   Как вас
    зову́т?
    My name is. . . .   Меня́
    зову́т. . . .

newspaper   газе́та, газе́ты
    (pl.)
nine   де́вять
nineteen   девятна́дцать
ninety   девяно́сто
ninth   девя́тый
no   нет
Not this one; that one!   Не э́ту,
    а ту!
November   ноя́брь
number   но́мер

O

o'clock   час
October   октя́брь
OK   хорошо́
on   на
one   оди́н
only   то́лько
opera glasses   бино́кль
or   и́ли
orchestra   парте́р
order (v.)   заказа́ть
our   на́ши
over there   вон там

P

Palace of Congresses   Дворе́ц
    съе́здов
park   парк
pass (n.)   про́пуск, про́пуски
    (pl.)
passport   па́спорт, паспорта́
    (pl.)
pay (v.)   плати́ть
Pay!   Плати́те.
place (n.)   ме́сто, места́ (pl.)
please   пожа́луйста
postcard   откры́тка,
    откры́тки (pl.)
post office   по́чта
pound   фунт, фу́нты (pl.)
price   цена́
program   програ́мка,
    програ́мки (pl.)

R

receipt квита́нция, чек
red кра́сное
Red Square Кра́сная
  пло́щадь
Repeat! Повтори́те.
restaurant рестора́н
restroom туале́т, туале́ты
  (pl.)
  ladies' room же́нский
    туале́т
  men's room мужско́й
    туале́т
ride (v.) е́хать
right
  right side пра́вая сторона́
  to the right напра́во
right away сейча́с
ring я́рус
  first ring пе́рвый я́рус
  second ring второ́й я́рус
(room) number но́мер
Rossiya (hotel) Росси́я
row ряд
ruble рубль, рубли́ (pl.)

S

salami колбаса́
  with salami с колбасо́й
sandwich бутербро́д,
  бутербро́ды (pl.)
Saturday суббо́та
screwdriver (drink) во́дка с
  со́ком
seat ме́сто, места́ (pl.)
See! Уви́дите.
second второ́й
semidry полусухо́е
send (v.) посла́ть
September сентя́брь
Service Bureau Бюро́
  обслу́живания
seven семь
seventeen семна́дцать
seventh седьмо́й
seventy се́мьдесят
Sheremetyevo (airport)
  Шереме́тьево

show
  Show me! Покажи́те мне.
  I'll show you. Я покажу́.
Sign! Распиши́тесь.
six шесть
sixteen шестна́дцать
sixth шесто́й
sixty шестьдеся́т
slower ме́дленнее
smoke (v.) кури́ть
  no smoking Не кури́ть
smorgasbord шве́дский стол
snack bar буфе́т
soft drink лимона́д
Sokolniki Соко́льники
souvenir сувени́р, сувени́ры
  (pl.)
speak
  I speak Russian. Я говорю́
    по-ру́сски.
Sportivnaya station
  Спорти́вная
stamp ма́рка, ма́рки (pl.)
station ста́нция
  To which station? До како́й
    ста́нции?
straight пря́мо
subway метро́
sugar са́хар
  with sugar с са́харом
  without sugar без са́хара
Sunday воскресе́нье

T

Take! Возьми́те.
  I'll take. Я возьму́.
taxi такси́
tea чай
telephone телефо́н
Tell me. Скажи́те.
ten де́сять
tenth деся́тый
thank you спаси́бо
  thank you very much
    спаси́бо большо́е, большо́е
    спаси́бо
theater теа́тр
then тогда́, пото́м
there там

they они́
third тре́тий
thirteen трина́дцать
thirty три́дцать
this э́то
  Not this, but that. Не э́ту, а ту.
three три
Thursday четве́рг
ticket биле́т, биле́ты *(pl.)*
time
  For what time? На како́е вре́мя?
to в, на
  (to) there туда́
today сего́дня
tomorrow за́втра
  for tomorrow на за́втра
tonic то́ник
Tuesday вто́рник
twelve двена́дцать
twenty два́дцать
two два *(m.),* две *(f.)*

U

unfortunately к сожале́нию
University station Университе́тская

V

vodka во́дка

W

wait ждать
Wait! Сто́йте.

Waiter! Молодо́й челове́к.
Waitress! Де́вушка.
want
  I want. Я хочу́.
  Do you want? Вы хоти́те?
water вода́
Wednesday среда́
what что
  What else? Что ещё?
when когда́
where где
where to куда́
which како́й
white бе́лое
(he, she) will, (you)
  will бу́дет, бу́дете *(pl.)*
wine вино́
Winston Ви́нстон
wrap *(v.)* заверну́ть
write
  Write out an order.
  Вы́пишите.
  Write it down. Напиши́те.

Y

yes да
yesterday вчера́
you вы, вам, вас
you'll see уви́дите
young man молодо́й челове́к
your ваш *(m.),* ва́ша *(f.),* ва́ше *(neut.),* ва́ши *(pl.)*
You're welcome.
  Пожа́луйста.

ITINERARY

DATE	PLACE

EXPENSES

DATE	AMT.	U.S.$	FOR:

PURCHASES

ITEM _____

WHERE BOUGHT _____

GIFT FOR _____COST_____U.S.$_____

ITEM _____

WHERE BOUGHT _____

GIFT FOR _____COST_____U.S.$_____

ITEM _____

WHERE BOUGHT _____

GIFT FOR _____COST_____U.S.$_____

ITEM _____

WHERE BOUGHT _____

GIFT FOR _____COST_____U.S.$_____

ITEM _____

WHERE BOUGHT _____

GIFT FOR _____COST_____U.S.$_____

ADDRESSES

NAME _____

ADDRESS _____

_____ PHONE _____

NAME _____

ADDRESS _____

_____ PHONE _____

NAME _____

ADDRESS _____

_____ PHONE _____

NAME _____

ADDRESS _____

_____ PHONE _____

NAME _____

ADDRESS _____

_____ PHONE _____

TRAVEL DIARY

DATE_____

DATE_____

DATE_____

DATE_____

DATE_____

DATE_____

DATE_____